3 1389 02071 5850

E
Star
12/11

3.49

A Note to Parents

D0660063

DK READERS is a compellin
readers, designed in conjunct
experts, including Dr. Linda (
tion
at Clemson University. Dr. Gu
has served as President
of the National Reading Conference and the College Reading Association, and has recently been elected to serve as President of the International Reading Association.

Beautiful illustrations and superb full-color photographs combine with engaging, easy-to-read stories to offer a fresh approach to each subject in the series. Each DK READER is guaranteed to capture a child's interest while developing his or her reading skills, general knowledge, and love of reading.

The five levels of DK READERS are aimed at different reading abilities, enabling you to choose the books that are exactly right for your child:

Pre-level 1: Learning to read
Level 1: Beginning to read
Level 2: Beginning to read alone
Level 3: Reading alone
Level 4: Proficient readers

The "normal" age at which a child begins to read can be anywhere from three to eight years old. Adult participation through the lower levels is very helpful for providing encouragement, discussing storylines, and sounding out unfamiliar words.

No matter which level you select, you can be sure that you are helping your child learn to read, then read to learn!

LONDON, NEW YORK, MUNICH,
MELBOURNE, AND DELHI

For Dorling Kindersley
Senior Editor Laura Gilbert
Managing Art Editor Ron Stobbart
Publishing Manager Catherine Saunders
Art Director Lisa Lanzarini
Associate Publisher Simon Beecroft
Category Publisher Alex Allan
Production Editor Sean Daly
Production Controller Rita Sinha
Reading Consultant Dr. Linda Gambrell

For Lucasfilm
Executive Editor J. W. Rinzler
Art Director Troy Alders
Keeper of the Holocron Leland Chee
Director of Publishing Carol Roeder

Designed and edited by Tall Tree Ltd
Designer Sandra Perry
Editor Jon Richards

First published in the United States in 2011
by DK Publishing
375 Hudson Street, New York, New York 10014

11 12 13 14 15 10 9 8 7 6 5 4 3

Copyright © 2011 Lucasfilm Ltd and ™
All rights reserved. Used under authorization.
Page design copyright © 2011 Dorling Kinderley Limited

003—178076—04/2011

All rights reserved under International and Pan-American Copyright Conventions. No part of this publication may be reproduced, stored in a retrieval system, or transmitted in any form or by any means, electronic, mechanical, photocopying, recording, or otherwise, without the prior written permission of the copyright owner.
Published in Great Britain by Dorling Kindersley Limited

DK books are available at special discounts when purchased in bulk for sales promotions, premiums, fund-raising, or educational use.
For details, contact:
DK Publishing Special Markets
375 Hudson Street
New York, New York 10014
SpecialSales@dk.com

A catalog record for this book is available from the Library of Congress.

ISBN: 978-0-7566-8279-8 (Paperback)
ISBN: 978-0-7566-8278-1 (Hardback)

Reproduced by Media Development and Printing Ltd., UK
Printed and bound in China by L.Rex Printing Company Ltd.

Discover more at:

www.dk.com
www.starwars.com

Contents

4 Introduction
6 Zillo Beast
8 Gutkurrs
10 Kwazel maw
12 Rishi eel
14 Gundark
16 Skalder
18 Mastiff phalone
20 Narglatch
22 Shaaks
24 Xandu
26 Aiwha
28 Roggwart
30 Friends and monsters
32 Glossary

DK READERS

LEARNING TO READ

pre-level 1

STAR WARS®

THE CLONE WARS™

Don't Wake the Zillo Beast!

Jon Richards

Watch your step!
Some creatures are
friendly.
Other creatures are
dangerous.

Zillo (ZIL-LOH) Beast

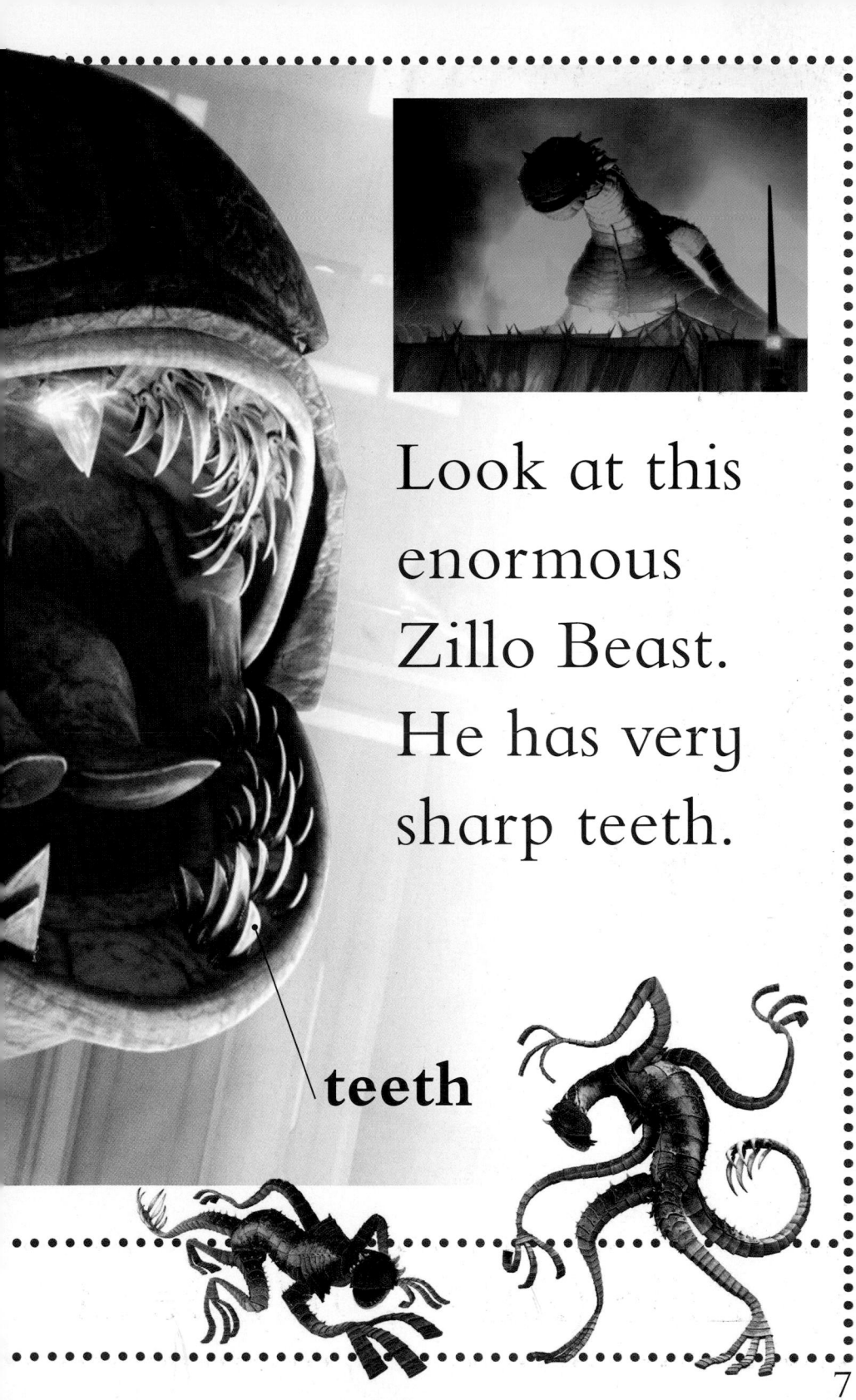

Look at this enormous Zillo Beast. He has very sharp teeth.

Look at these
hungry gutkurrs.

gutkurrs (GUT-CURS)

They have spikes on their backs.

kwazel maw (KWAY-ZELL MOR)

leg

Look at this
Rishi eel.

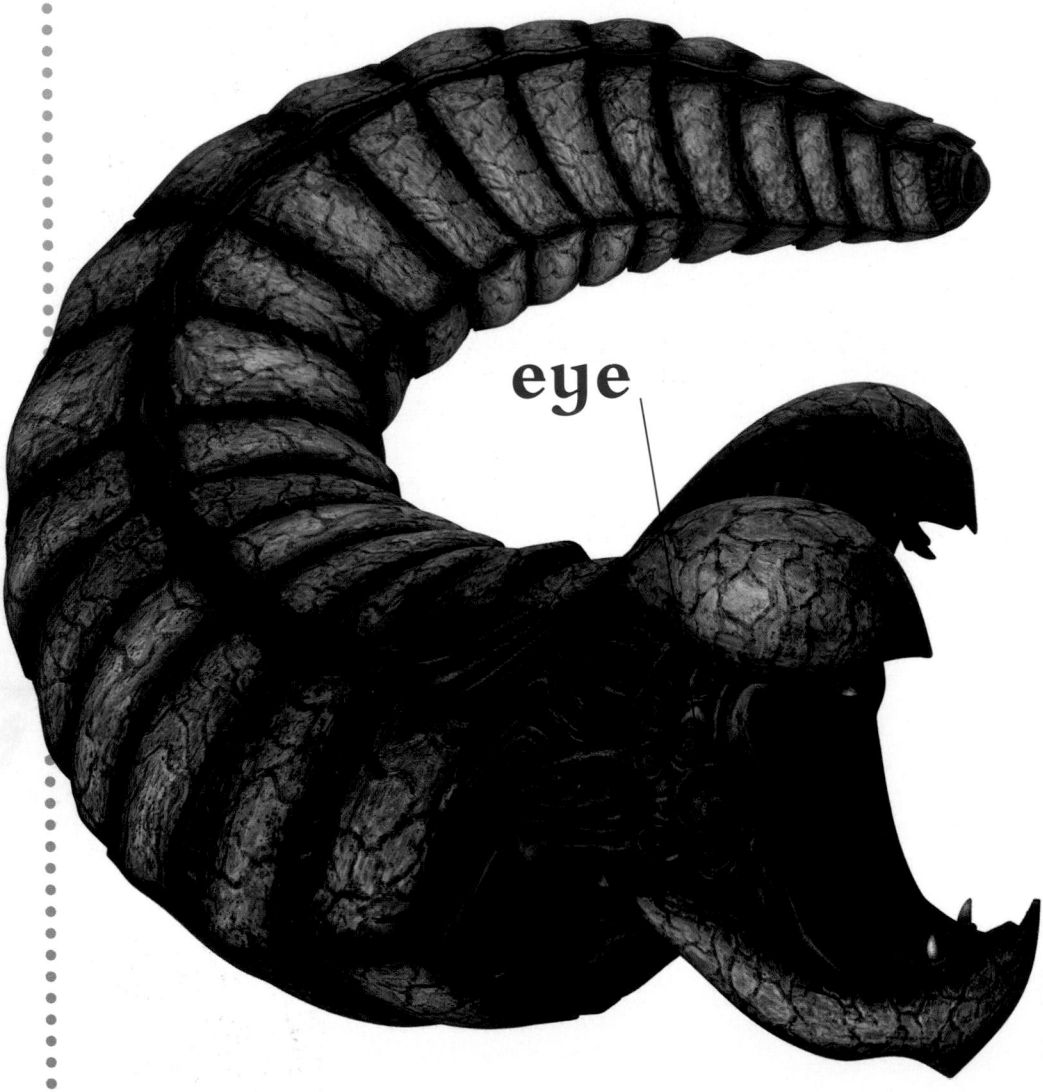

Rishi (REE-SHEE) eel

It lives inside dark holes on a cold moon.

Look at this angry gundark.
It has four very strong arms.

gundark (GUN-DARK)

arms

skalder (SKOLL-DER)

Look at this
huge skalder.
It has very
thick skin.
thick skin

mastiff phalone
(MASS-TIFF FAA-LOAN)

It has a sharp, pointed beak.

narglatch (NAR-GLATCH)

Look at this spiky
narglatch.
It lives on an icy moon.

Look at these peaceful shaaks.

shaaks (SHOCKS)

They live in groups called herds.

Look at this flying xandu. It flaps its powerful wings.

xandu (ZAN-DOO)

wings
Anakin Skywalker

aiwha (A-WAH)

Look at this massive aiwha. It can fly through the air.

Look at this
scary roggwart.
It has sharp claws
and robot arms.

roggwart (ROG-WORT)

Now you have met the creatures.

Which is your favorite?

Glossary

Herds
large groups of animals

Marks
patterns on an animal's skin

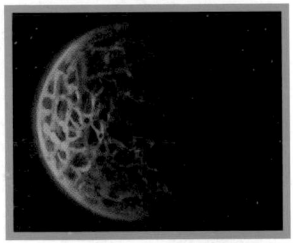

Moon
a small object that goes around a planet

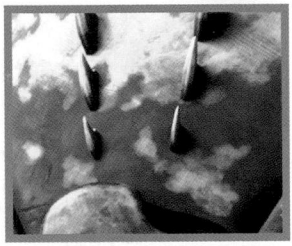

Spikes
pointed parts of the body

Teeth
parts of the body that are used to bite and chew food